My dearest friend Janice
To

Viv
From

Christmas '98
Date

WISDOM
FOR A
WOMAN'S
HEART

WISDOM FOR A WOMAN'S HEART

■ ■

COPYRIGHT © 1996 BY GARBORG'S HEART 'N HOME, INC.

PUBLISHED BY GARBORG'S HEART 'N HOME, INC.

P.O. BOX 20132, BLOOMINGTON, MN 55420

❧

ALL TEXT IN THIS BOOK HAS BEEN TAKEN FROM *THE MESSAGE* © BY
EUGENE H. PETERSON, 1996. ALL RIGHTS RESERVED. PUBLISHED BY PERMISSION
OF NAVPRESS, P.O. BOX 35001, COLORADO SPRINGS, CO 80933, AND IN
ASSOCIATION WITH THE LITERARY AGENCY OF ALIVE COMMUNICATIONS, INC.,
1465 KELLY JOHNSON BLVD., SUITE 320, COLORADO SPRINGS, CO 80920.

❧

ART: HALE, PHILIP LESLIE. *THE CRIMSON RAMBLER.*

ART WORK FROM WOOD RIVER GALLERY

MILL VALLEY, CALIFORNIA

❧

ISBN 1-881830-38-1

❧

WISDOM FOR A WOMAN'S HEART

The Message is a contemporary rendering of the Bible from the original languages, crafted to present its tone, rhythm, events, and ideas in everyday speech.

YOUR GOD-CREATED IDENTITY

*L*ive out your God-created identity.
Live generously and graciously toward others,
the way God lives toward you.

■ ■ ■ ■ ■ ■ ■ ■ ■ ■ ■ ■ ■ ■

Matthew 5:48

WISDOM

Take your everyday, ordinary life—your sleeping, eating, going-to-work, and walking-around life—and place it before God as an offering. Embracing what God does for you is the best thing you can do for him. Don't become so well-adjusted to your culture that you fit into it without even thinking. Instead, fix your attention on God. You'll be changed from the inside out. Readily recognize what he wants from you, and quickly respond to it.

Romans 12:1-2

WISDOM

There is far more to your inner life than the food you put in your stomach, more to your outer appearance than the clothes you hang on your body. Look at the ravens, free and unfettered, not tied down to a job description, carefree in the care of God. And you count far more.

WISDOM

Has anyone by fussing before the mirror ever gotten taller by so much as an inch? If fussing can't even do that, why fuss at all? Walk into the fields and look at the wildflowers. They don't fuss with their appearance—but have you ever seen color and design quite like it? The ten best-dressed men and women in the country look shabby alongside them. If God gives such attention to the wildflowers, most of them never even seen, don't you think he'll attend to you, take pride in you, do his best for you?...

WISDOM

Steep yourself in God-reality,
God-initiative, God-provisions.
You'll find all your everyday human
concerns will be met. Don't be afraid
of missing out. You're my dearest friends!
The Father wants to give you the
very kingdom itself.

WISDOM

Be generous. Give to the poor. Get yourselves a bank that can't go bankrupt, a bank in heaven far from bankrobbers, safe from embezzlers, a bank you can bank on. It's obvious, isn't it? The place where your treasure is, is the place you will most want to be, and end up being.

■ ■ ■ ■ ■ ■ ■ ■ ■ ■ ■ ■ ■ ■

Luke 12:23-28,31-32

WISDOM

What happens when we live God's way? He brings gifts into our lives, much the same way that fruit appears in an orchard—things like affection for others, exuberance about life, serenity. We develop a willingness to stick with things, a sense of compassion in the heart, and a conviction that a basic holiness permeates things and people. We find ourselves involved in loyal commitments, not needing to force our way in life, able to marshal and direct our energies wisely....

WISDOM

$\mathcal{S}$ince this is the kind of life we have chosen, the life of the Spirit, let us make sure that we do not just hold it as an idea in our heads or a sentiment in our hearts, but work out its implications in every detail of our lives. That means we will not compare ourselves with each other as if one of us were better and another worse. We have far more interesting things to do with our lives. Each of us is an original.

▪ ▪ ▪ ▪ ▪ ▪ ▪ ▪ ▪ ▪ ▪ ▪ ▪

Galatians 5:22-23,25-26

WISDOM

It's in Christ that we find out who we are
and what we are living for. Long before we first
heard of Christ and got our hopes up, he had
his eye on us, had designs on us for glorious
living, part of the overall purpose he is
working out in everything and everyone.

■ ■ ■ ■ ■ ■ ■ ■ ■ ■ ■ ■ ■

Ephesians 1:11

WISDOM

WISDOM

$\mathcal{N}$o one lights a lamp, then hides it in a drawer. It's put on a lamp stand so those entering the room have light to see where they're going. Your eye is a lamp, lighting up your whole body. If you live wide-eyed in wonder and belief, your body fills up with light.... Keep your eyes open, your lamp burning, so you don't get musty and murky. Keep your life as well-lighted as your best-lighted room.

■ ■ ■ ■ ■ ■ ■ ■ ■ ■ ■ ■ ■

Luke 11:33-36

WISDOM

𝒫ursue a righteous life—a life of wonder,
faith, love, steadiness, courtesy. Run hard
and fast in the faith. Seize the eternal life,
the life you were called to, the life you
so fervently embraced.

■ ■ ■ ■ ■ ■ ■ ■ ■ ■ ■ ■ ■

1 Timothy 6:11-12

𝒞elebrate God all day, every day.
I mean, *revel* in him!

■ ■ ■ ■ ■ ■ ■ ■ ■ ■ ■ ■ ■

Philippians 4:4

WISDOM

$\mathcal{N}$ow you're dressed in a new wardrobe.
Every item of your new way of life is
custom-made by the Creator, with his label
on it. All the old fashions are now obsolete....
From now on everyone is defined by Christ,
everyone is included in Christ.

WISDOM

So, chosen by God for this new life of love,
dress in the wardrobe God picked out for
you: compassion, kindness, humility,
quiet strength, discipline.

Be even-tempered, content with second place,
quick to forgive an offense. Forgive as quickly
and completely as the Master forgave you.
And regardless of what else you put on,
wear love. It's your basic, all-purpose
garment. Never be without it.

■ ■ ■ ■ ■ ■ ■ ■ ■ ■ ■ ■ ■

Colossians 3:10-14

WISDOM

You know me inside and out,
you know every bone in my body;
You know exactly how I was made, bit by bit,
how I was sculpted from nothing
into something.
Like an open book, you watched me
grow from conception to birth;
all the stages of my life were
spread out before you,
The days of my life all prepared
before I'd even lived one day.

WISDOM

Your thoughts—how rare, how beautiful!
God, I'll never comprehend them!
I couldn't even begin to count them—
any more than I could count the
sand of the sea.
Oh, let me rise in the morning and
live always with you!

■ ■ ■ ■ ■ ■ ■ ■ ■ ■ ■ ■ ■ ■

Psalm 139:15-18

WISDOM

GOD'S
EXTRAVAGANT
WISDOM

Have you ever come on anything quite like this extravagant generosity of God, this deep, deep wisdom? It's way over our heads. We'll never figure it out.

"Is there anyone around who can explain God? Anyone smart enough to tell him what to do? Anyone who has done him such a huge favor that God has to ask his advice?"

WISDOM

Everything comes from him;
Everything happens through him;
Everything ends up in him.
Always glory! Always praise!

■ ■ ■ ■ ■ ■ ■ ■ ■ ■ ■ ■ ■ ■

Romans 11:33-36

WISDOM

We never really know enough until we
recognize that God alone knows it all.

■ ■ ■ ■ ■ ■ ■ ■ ■ ■ ■ ■ ■ ■

1 Corinthians 8:3

WISDOM

This Christian life is a great mystery, far
exceeding our understanding, but some
things are clear enough:
He appeared in a human body,
was proved right by the invisible Spirit,
was seen by angels.
He was proclaimed among all kinds of peoples,
believed in all over the world,
taken up into heavenly glory.

■ ■ ■ ■ ■ ■ ■ ■ ■ ■ ■ ■ ■

1 Timothy 3:16

WISDOM

We, of course, have plenty of wisdom to pass on to you once you get your feet on firm spiritual ground, but it's not popular wisdom, the fashionable wisdom of high-priced experts that will be out-of-date in a year or so. God's wisdom is something mysterious that goes deep into the interior of his purposes. You don't find it lying around on the surface. It's not the latest message, but more like the oldest—what God determined as the way to bring out his best in us, long before we ever arrived on the scene....

WISDOM

That's why we have this Scripture text:
"No one's ever seen or heard anything like this,
Never so much as imagined anything
quite like it—
What God has arranged for those
who love him."

■ ■ ■ ■ ■ ■ ■ ■ ■ ■ ■ ■ ■ ■

1 Corinthians 2:6-9

WISDOM

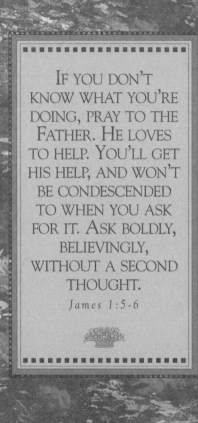

IF YOU DON'T
KNOW WHAT YOU'RE
DOING, PRAY TO THE
FATHER. HE LOVES
TO HELP. YOU'LL GET
HIS HELP, AND WON'T
BE CONDESCENDED
TO WHEN YOU ASK
FOR IT. ASK BOLDLY,
BELIEVINGLY,
WITHOUT A SECOND
THOUGHT.

James 1:5-6

$\mathcal{W}$hat a wildly wonderful world, GOD!
You made it all, with Wisdom at your side,
made earth overflow with your
wonderful creations.
Oh, look—the deep, wide sea,
brimming with fish past counting....

WISDOM

All the creatures look expectantly to you
to give them their meals on time.
You come, and they gather around;
you open your hand and they eat from it.
If you turned your back,
they'd die in a minute—

$\mathcal{T}$ake back your Spirit and they die,
revert to original mud;
Send out your Spirit and they spring to life—
the whole countryside in bloom and blossom.
The glory of GOD—let it last forever!
Let GOD enjoy his creation!

■ ■ ■ ■ ■ ■ ■ ■ ■ ■ ■ ■ ■

Psalm 104:24-25,27-31

WISDOM

To us who are personally called by God himself...Christ is God's ultimate miracle and wisdom all wrapped up in one. Human wisdom is so tinny, so impotent, next to the seeming absurdity of God. Human strength can't begin to compete with God's "weakness."

■ ■ ■ ■ ■ ■ ■ ■ ■ ■ ■ ■ ■

1 Corinthians 1:24-25

All our praise is focused through Jesus on this incomparably wise God!

■ ■ ■ ■ ■ ■ ■ ■ ■ ■ ■ ■ ■

Romans 16:27

WISDOM

What you say goes, GOD,
and *stays*, as permanent as the heavens.
Your truth never goes out of fashion;
it's as up-to-date as the earth when
the sun comes up.
Your Word and truth are dependable as ever;
that's what you ordered—you set
the earth going.

WISDOM

I would have given up when the
hard times came.
But I'll never forget the advice you gave me;
you saved my life with those wise words.
Save me! I'm all yours.
I look high and low for your words of wisdom.

■ ■ ■ ■ ■ ■ ■ ■ ■ ■ ■ ■ ■ ■

Psalm 119:89-94

WISDOM

You are right and you *do* right, GOD;
your decisions are right on target.
You rightly instruct us in how to live
ever faithful to you....

WISDOM

Your righteousness is eternally right,
your revelation is the only truth.
Even though troubles came down on me hard,
your commands always gave me delight.
The way you tell me to live is always right;
help me understand it so I can live
to the fullest.

■ ■ ■ ■ ■ ■ ■ ■ ■ ■ ■ ■ ■ ■

Psalm 119:137-138,142-144

WISDOM

THE WAY
TO JOY

The revelation of GOD is whole
and pulls our lives together.
The signposts of GOD are clear
and point out the right road.
The life-maps of GOD are right,
showing the way to joy.
The directions of GOD are plain
and easy on the eyes.

WISDOM

God's reputation is twenty-four carat gold,
with a lifetime guarantee.
The decisions of God are accurate
down to the nth degree....
There's more: God's Word warns us of danger
and directs us to hidden treasure.
Otherwise how will we find our way?

■ ■ ■ ■ ■ ■ ■ ■ ■ ■ ■ ■

Psalm 19:7-9,11-12

WISDOM

$\mathcal{M}$ay the Master take you by the hand and
lead you along the path of God's love
and Christ's endurance.

■■■■■■■■■■■■■■

2 Thessalonians 3:5

WISDOM

We pray that you'll have the strength to stick it out over the long haul—not the grim strength of gritting your teeth but the glory-strength God gives. It is strength that endures the unendurable and spills over into joy, thanking the Father who makes us strong enough to take part in everything bright and beautiful that he has for us.

■ ■ ■ ■ ■ ■ ■ ■ ■ ■ ■ ■ ■

Colossians 1:11-12

WISDOM

You're blessed when you stay on course,
walking steadily on the road revealed by GOD.
You're blessed when you follow his directions,
doing your best to find him.
That's right—you don't go off on your own;
you walk straight along the road he set.

WISDOM

You, God, prescribed the right way to live;
now you expect us to live it.
Oh, that my steps might be steady,
keeping to the course you set;
Then I'd never have any regrets
in comparing my life with your counsel.

■ ■ ■ ■ ■ ■ ■ ■ ■ ■ ■ ■ ■ ■

Psalm 119:1-6

WISDOM

$\mathcal{G}$ood friend, follow your father's
good advice;
don't wander off from your mother's teachings.
Wrap yourself in them from head to foot;
wear them like a scarf around your neck.
Wherever you walk, they'll guide you;
whenever you rest, they'll guard you.

■ ■ ■ ■ ■ ■ ■ ■ ■ ■ ■ ■ ■

Proverbs 6:20-22

WISDOM

So be content with who you are, and don't put on airs. God's strong hand is on you; he'll promote you at the right time. Live carefree before God; he is most careful with you.

■ ■ ■ ■ ■ ■ ■ ■ ■ ■ ■ ■ ■

1 Peter 5:6-7

In simple humility, let our gardener, God, landscape you with the Word, making a salvation-garden of your life.

■ ■ ■ ■ ■ ■ ■ ■ ■ ■ ■ ■ ■

James 1:21

WISDOM

$\mathcal{W}$hat matters is not your outer
appearance—the styling of your hair, the
jewelry you wear, the cut of your clothes—
but your inner disposition.
Cultivate inner beauty, the gentle, gracious
kind that God delights in.

■ ■ ■ ■ ■ ■ ■ ■ ■ ■ ■ ■ ■

1 Peter 3:3-4

WISDOM

WISDOM

I'll run the course you lay out for me
if you'll just show me how.
GOD, teach me lessons for living
so I can stay the course.

WISDOM

Give me insight so I can do what
you tell me—
my whole life one long, obedient response.
Guide me down the road of your
commandments;
I love traveling this freeway!
Give me a bent for your words of wisdom.

■ ■ ■ ■ ■ ■ ■ ■ ■ ■ ■ ■ ■

Psalm 119:32-36

WISDOM

$\mathcal{I}$'m happy from the inside out....
Now you've got my feet on the life path,
all radiant from the shining of your face.
Ever since you took my hand,
I'm on the right way.

■ ■ ■ ■ ■ ■ ■ ■ ■ ■ ■ ■ ■

Psalm 16:9,11

WISDOM

$\mathcal{O}$h, I'll guard with my life what you've
revealed to me,
guard it now, guard it ever;
And I'll stride freely through wide open spaces
as I look for your truth and your wisdom....
I cherish your commandments—
oh, how I love them!—
relishing every fragment of your counsel.

■ ■ ■ ■ ■ ■ ■ ■ ■ ■ ■ ■ ■ ■

Psalm 119:44-45,47-48

WISDOM

Every desirable and beneficial gift comes out of heaven. The gifts are rivers of light cascading down from the Father of Light.

■ ■ ■ ■ ■ ■ ■ ■ ■ ■ ■ ■ ■

James 1:17

WISDOM

*S*umming it all up, friends, I'd say you'll do best by filling your minds and meditating on things true, noble, reputable, authentic, compelling, gracious—the best, not the worst; the beautiful, not the ugly; things to praise, not things to curse.... Do that, and God, who makes everything work together, will work you into his most excellent harmonies.

Philippians 4:8-9

WISDOM

IN TUNE
WITH
EACH
OTHER

*L*et the peace of Christ keep you in tune
with each other, in step with each other.
None of this going off and doing your own
thing. And cultivate thankfulness.

■ ■ ■ ■ ■ ■ ■ ■ ■ ■ ■ ■ ■

Colossians 3:15

WISDOM

Real wisdom, God's wisdom, begins with a holy life and is characterized by getting along with others. It is gentle and reasonable, overflowing with mercy and blessings.

■ ■ ■ ■ ■ ■ ■ ■ ■ ■ ■ ■ ■ ■

James 3:17

WISDOM

An obedient, God-willed life is spacious.
Fear-of-GOD is a school in skilled living—
first you learn humility, then you
experience glory.

▪▪▪▪▪▪▪▪▪▪▪▪▪

Proverbs 15:32-33

WISDOM

$\mathscr{T}$his is my prayer: that your love will flourish and that you will not only love much but well. Learn to love appropriately. You need to use your head and test your feelings so that your love is sincere and intelligent, not sentimental gush.

■ ■ ■ ■ ■ ■ ■ ■ ■ ■ ■ ■ ■

Philippians 1:9-10

WISDOM

*G*ive away your life; you'll find life given back, but not merely given back—given back with bonus and blessing. Giving, not getting, is the way. Generosity begets generosity.

■ ■ ■ ■ ■ ■ ■ ■ ■ ■ ■ ■ ■

Luke 6:38

WISDOM

The world of the generous gets
larger and larger;
the world of the stingy gets smaller and smaller.
The one who blesses others is
abundantly blessed;
those who help others are helped.

■ ■ ■ ■ ■ ■ ■ ■ ■ ■ ■ ■ ■ ■

Proverbs 11:24-25

WISDOM

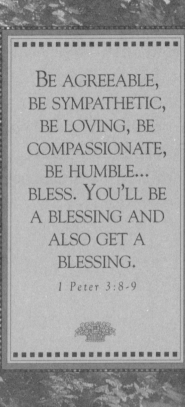

BE AGREEABLE,
BE SYMPATHETIC,
BE LOVING, BE
COMPASSIONATE,
BE HUMBLE...
BLESS. YOU'LL BE
A BLESSING AND
ALSO GET A
BLESSING.

1 Peter 3:8-9

$\mathcal{I}$'ve loved you the way my Father has loved me. Make yourselves at home in my love. If you keep my commands, you'll remain intimately at home in my love. That's what I've done—kept my Father's commands and made myself at home in his love.

■ ■ ■ ■ ■ ■ ■ ■ ■ ■ ■ ■ ■

John 15:9-10

WISDOM

The law code...finally adds up to this:
Love other people as well as you do yourself.
You can't go wrong when you love others.
When you add up everything in the
law code, the sum total is love.

■ ■ ■ ■ ■ ■ ■ ■ ■ ■ ■ ■ ■

Romans 13:9-10

WISDOM

I want you woven into a tapestry of love, in touch with everything there is to know of God. Then you will have minds confident and at rest, focused on Christ, God's great mystery. All the richest treasures of wisdom and knowledge are embedded in that mystery and nowhere else.

■■■■■■■■■■■■■

Colossians 2:2-3

WISDOM

$\mathcal{W}$orship the Lord your God and only
the Lord your God. Serve him with
absolute single-heartedness.

▪▪▪▪▪▪▪▪▪▪▪▪▪

Luke 4:8

$\mathcal{G}$od is one and there is no other. And
loving him with all passion and intelligence
and energy, and loving others as well as you
love yourself. Why, that's better than all
offerings and sacrifices put together!

▪▪▪▪▪▪▪▪▪▪▪▪▪

Mark 12:32-33

WISDOM

Watch what God does, and then you do it,
like children who learn proper behavior from
their parents. Mostly what God does is love you.
Keep company with him and learn a life of love.
Observe how Christ loved us. His love was not
cautious but extravagant. He didn't love in order
to get something from us but to give everything
of himself to us. Love like that.

∎∎∎∎∎∎∎∎∎∎∎∎∎

Ephesians 5:1-2

WISDOM

The one who plants in response to God,
letting God's Spirit do the growth work in him,
harvests a crop of real life, eternal life.
So let's not allow ourselves to get fatigued doing
good. At the right time we will harvest a good
crop if we don't give up, or quit.

■ ■ ■ ■ ■ ■ ■ ■ ■ ■ ■ ■ ■ ■

Galatians 6:8-9

WISDOM

Share what you have with others. God takes particular pleasure in acts of worship—a different kind of "sacrifice"—that take place in kitchen and workplace and on the streets.

■ ■ ■ ■ ■ ■ ■ ■ ■ ■ ■ ■ ■ ■ ■

Hebrews 13:16

WISDOM

$\mathcal{B}$e generous with the different things
God gave you, passing them around so all get
in on it: if words, let it be God's words; if help,
let it be God's hearty help. That way, God's
bright presence will be evident in everything
through Jesus, and he'll get all the credit
as the One mighty in everything—
encores to the end of time.

■ ■ ■ ■ ■ ■ ■ ■ ■ ■ ■ ■ ■

1 Peter 4:10-11

WISDOM

WISE
SAYINGS

These are the wise sayings of Solomon,
David's son, Israel's king—
Written down so we'll know how
to live well and right,
to understand what life means
and where it's going;
A manual for living,
for learning what's right and just and fair....
Start with GOD—the first step in learning
is bowing down to GOD.

▪ ▪ ▪ ▪ ▪ ▪ ▪ ▪ ▪ ▪ ▪ ▪ ▪ ▪

Proverbs 1:1-3,7

WISDOM

$\mathcal{P}$ay close attention, friend, to what your
father tells you;
never forget what you learned at your
mother's knee.
Wear their counsel like flowers in your hair,
like rings on your fingers.

■ ■ ■ ■ ■ ■ ■ ■ ■ ■ ■ ■ ■ ■

Proverbs 1:8-9

WISDOM

Trust GOD from the bottom of your heart;
don't try to figure out everything on your own.
Listen for GOD's voice in everything you do,
everywhere you go;
he's the one who will keep you on track.
Don't assume that you know it all.
Run to GOD!

■ ■ ■ ■ ■ ■ ■ ■ ■ ■ ■ ■ ■

Proverbs 3:5-7

WISDOM

*D*ear friend, guard Clear Thinking and
Common Sense with your life;
don't for a minute lose sight of them.
They'll keep your soul alive and well,
they'll keep you fit and attractive.

■ ■ ■ ■ ■ ■ ■ ■ ■ ■ ■ ■ ■ ■

Proverbs 3:21-26

WISDOM

I [Wisdom] love those who love me;
those who look for me find me.
Wealth and Glory accompany me...
Handing out life to those who love me,
filling their arms with life—armloads of life!...

WISDOM

Blessed the man, blessed the woman,
who listens to me,
awake and ready for me each morning,
alert and responsive as I start my day's work.
When you find me, you find life, real life,
to say nothing of God's good pleasure.

■ ■ ■ ■ ■ ■ ■ ■ ■ ■ ■ ■ ■ ■

Proverbs 8:17-18,21,34-35

WISDOM

$\mathscr{B}$lessings accrue on a good and honest life...
A good and honest life is a blessed memorial....
GOD's blessing makes life rich;
nothing we do can improve on GOD.

■■■■■■■■■■■■■

Proverbs 10:6-7,22

WISDOM

The Fear-of-GOD builds up confidence,
and makes a world safe for your children.
The Fear-of-GOD is a spring of living water.

■ ■ ■ ■ ■ ■ ■ ■ ■ ■ ■ ■ ■

Proverbs 14:26-27

Knowing what is right is like
deep water in the heart;
a wise person draws from the well within.

■ ■ ■ ■ ■ ■ ■ ■ ■ ■ ■ ■ ■

Proverbs 20:5

WISDOM

$\mathcal{A}$ wise person gets known for insight;
gracious words add to one's reputation.

■ ■ ■ ■ ■ ■ ■ ■ ■ ■ ■ ■ ■

Proverbs 16:21

$\mathcal{W}$ell-spoken words bring satisfaction;
well-done work has its own reward.

■ ■ ■ ■ ■ ■ ■ ■ ■ ■ ■ ■ ■

Proverbs 12:14

WISDOM

WISDOM

*F*riends love through all kinds of weather,
and families stick together in
all kinds of trouble.

■ ■ ■ ■ ■ ■ ■ ■ ■ ■ ■ ■ ■ ■

Proverbs 17:17

*G*od-loyal people, living honest lives,
make it much easier for their children.

■ ■ ■ ■ ■ ■ ■ ■ ■ ■ ■ ■ ■ ■

Proverbs 20:7

WISDOM

*W*ise men and women are always learning,
always listening for fresh insights.

■ ■ ■ ■ ■ ■ ■ ■ ■ ■ ■ ■ ■ ■

Proverbs 18:15

*T*ake good counsel and accept correction—
that's the way to live wisely and well.

■ ■ ■ ■ ■ ■ ■ ■ ■ ■ ■ ■ ■ ■

Proverbs 19:20

WISDOM

*D*rinking from the beautiful chalice
of knowledge
is better than adorning oneself
with gold and rare gems.

▪▪▪▪▪▪▪▪▪▪▪▪

Proverbs 20:15

A sterling reputation is better
than striking it rich;
a gracious spirit is better than
money in the bank.

▪▪▪▪▪▪▪▪▪▪▪▪

Proverbs 22:1

WISDOM

$\mathcal{F}$orm your purpose by asking for counsel,
then carry it out using all the help you can get.

■ ■ ■ ■ ■ ■ ■ ■ ■ ■ ■ ■ ■

Proverbs 20:18

$\mathcal{T}$he very steps we take come from GOD;
otherwise how would we know
where we're going?

■ ■ ■ ■ ■ ■ ■ ■ ■ ■ ■ ■ ■

Proverbs 20:24

WISDOM

The right word at the right time
is like a custom-made piece of jewelry,
And a wise friend's timely reprimand
is like a gold ring slipped on your finger.

■ ■ ■ ■ ■ ■ ■ ■ ■ ■ ■ ■ ■ ■

Proverbs 25:11-12

WISDOM

$\mathscr{C}$harm can mislead and beauty soon fades.
The woman to be admired and praised
is the woman who lives in the Fear-of-GOD.

■ ■ ■ ■ ■ ■ ■ ■ ■ ■ ■ ■ ■ ■

Proverbs 31:30

WISDOM